THE SCHOOL OF LIFE is dedicated to exploring life's big questions: *How can we fulfill our potential? Can work be inspiring? Why does community matter? Can relationships last a lifetime?* We don't have all the answers, but we will direct you towards a variety of useful ideas—from philosophy to literature, psychology to the visual arts—that are guaranteed to stimulate, provoke, nourish and console.

THESCHOOLOFLIFE.COM

By the same author:

*Locke, Language and Early-Modern Philosophy*

By Thomas Hobbes:

*The Elements of Law*
*De Cive*
*Leviathan*

# HOBBES

Great Thinkers on Modern Life

## Hannah Dawson

PEGASUS BOOKS

NEW YORK  LONDON

HOBBES

Pegasus Books LLC
80 Broad Street, 5th Floor
New York, NY 10004

Copyright © 2015 by Hannah Dawson

First Pegasus Books edition 2015

ISBN: 978-1-60598-806-1

10 9 8 7 8 6 5 4 3 2 1

Printed in the United States of America
Distributed by W. W. Norton & Company, Inc.

*To Dora and Ada Eatwell*

# CONTENTS

# INTRODUCTION

..........

Thomas Hobbes is a hated man. He said that it is in our nature to be at war with each other, and that we need an all-powerful government to terrify us into submission. He therefore seems to be both depressing cynic and totalitarian apologist, seeing the worst in humanity and prescribing a chilling solution, a cure far more horrible than the disease, a place where all individual freedom is crushed by the irresistible might of the State – that great Leviathan, the beast of the deep green sea.

Why on earth, then, have I chosen him for this book? What could he, nasty, brutish Mr Hobbes, the 'Monster of Malmesbury', possibly have to teach us about how to live well? In a sense, it is precisely because of his gritty verdict on our human condition that we need to listen to him. While we do not want to let him take us all the way to the abyss of his authoritarian dystopia, we would do well to take note of his clear-eyed assessment of the psychological forces that pit us against one another, and the fact that, as uncomfortable as it is, we need to be restrained.

When I first read him at university, I was as awed as I was appalled. He made me ask certain fundamental questions which, I blush to remember, I had never really asked before. Why is it that human beings the world over tend to obey the law? What is the point of government? These are, Hobbes made me see for the first time, very odd phenomena. We are naturally free and equal, we do not as a rule like being told what to do, so what possible reason could we have for *agreeing* to be controlled by politicians, whose instructions chafe and who we do not generally like very much? Hobbes gives us the compelling answer: because it is in our interests. I can whistle about the streets or, indeed, in the office or at home, safe in the knowledge that I probably won't be hit or killed, in part at least because my would-be attackers are frightened of going to jail and therefore leave me alone. More broadly, there are a whole host of activities – monetary transactions, renting a house, motorway driving, even having a party – which are at a basic level dependent on the coercive apparatus of the State and the mutual trust and respect that this creates. This is the civilized and civilizing foundation without which the fantastically plural coordinations of society could not hope to get under way. It is on this foundation that I am free to make as much or as little of my life as I am able. This is why, Hobbes helped me to understand, I should obey and value government. As the first great social contract theorist, he shows us why we consent – even tacitly – to authority.

One might respond: most of us do not really consent to government. Even those who are lucky enough to line up at the polling booths every five years are participating in a mirage of democracy. The fact is that we are always under one government or another, and what we want seems often to bear very little relation to what they do. Far from choosing subjection, we are born into it, and so this tacit consent of Hobbes's looks rather like no consent at all.

But Hobbes sees this too, indeed more acutely than most. He knows that we are animals and that, as in the law of the jungle, might makes right. I often think of this when I am cycling through central London and a huge red bus is bearing down on me. It ought to give way, but that matters not a jot to what we both do: it cuts me up and I break to a halt, stranded and choking in its black smoke, but alive. The rights and wrongs of the situation are irrelevant. The driver and I both know that he is immensely more powerful than me, and that I will bend to his will. I let him rule me. So too, America, or any other enormously superior alpha male, does pretty much what he likes, even if, unlike most bus drivers, he dresses it up in gentle words.

What is so thrilling about Hobbes's analysis is that he sees the brute reality in the same breath as consent and agency. We are continually operated upon by all manner of circumstances and passions, but that does not mean that we are not free, that we do not have choices. In the case of government, the fact that some of us feel forced to obey, does not make it any less in our interests to do so, or indeed, any the less chosen. We all consent; it's just that there is a vast attitudinal spectrum of permission. The unreflective ones, who go around as Hobbes says with a magnifying glass, who wince at every intrusion and demand of the State, consent with a heavy heart, out of fear of their 'oppressor'. Whereas the enlightened, who have the binoculars of Hobbes's civil science to see far down the chain of cause and effect to the incomparable horror of what life would be like without the State and who know therefore what is at stake – they too consent out of fear, but in their case it is a fear of the war that would ensue without government to protect them. They consent therefore with a spring in their step. They know that they have been given an unnatural opportunity to pursue their dreams.

The lessons from Hobbes, however, go much further than the politics which have made him a household name. What he wants to teach us, in addition to how we can escape debilitating fear, is what it means to be free, and what it means to be good, to show us that – even at our most rational – we are pressed on by our desires, and that we must be ever watchful of the dangers of language and religion. Weaving its way through his philosophy is a deep sense, sometimes wretched, sometimes liberating, that, while we can and do reach out to other human beings, in the final analysis we are alone. Even if we violently disagree with Hobbes much or indeed most of the time, he can teach us to meditate more carefully than we are accustomed on the subjectivity, motivations and opinions which structure our lives.

Who was this man whose thoughts soared so high? According to his friend and admirer John Aubrey, who wrote about him in his wonderfully graphic *Brief Lives*, when Hobbes was deep in conversation his eyes 'shone', as if they had 'a bright live-coal within'; when he 'laughed, was witty, and in a merry humour', they scrunched up so tightly that 'one could scarce see his eyes'; and when 'by and by . . . he was serious and positive', they opened remarkably wide. This snapshot rings true to the intensely engaged and energetic personality that emanates from his writing, and is suggestive of the man who we know, from the dear friendships he nurtured throughout his long life, was as eager for sociability as he was for productive solitude.

Born in Malmesbury, Wiltshire, in 1588, Hobbes did not have a particularly auspicious start in life. His father was a 'drunken knave' of a clergyman. Forced to flee his parish for punching a neighbouring vicar while Hobbes was at Oxford, he seems to have disappeared from his son's life for ever. Thanks, however, to the vista of opportunity which university opened up for men of modest backgrounds in those years, Hobbes spent most of his ninety-one years as tutor, secretary and retainer of the Cavendish family – the rich earls of Devonshire – and as a provocative citizen of the European philosophical republic of letters.

Indeed, for the main part of his extraordinarily long adult life, his attention and writing were focused not on politics, but on the so-called scientific revolution, that highly diffuse 'movement' which self-consciously blew apart (though not without massive, often un-acknowledged, continuities) the largely Aristotelian view of the world that had dominated the intellectual Establishment. Aristotle had suggested that the world was made up of matter on the one hand, and substantial forms on the other – real, universal essences of substances such as men or horses which make them what they are. Hobbes was in the vanguard of the 'new philosophers' who proposed instead a mechanical universe. This threatened to drive a wedge between appearance and reality: if there are no longer specific essences out there in the world for the mind to grasp but only various arrangements of substance, then the 'essences' we perceive are made up by the mind rather than given by the world, and the qualities that seem to be 'in' things (heat and colour, for example) in fact bear no resemblance to those things themselves. Hobbes's approach took a particularly radical form: he was a materialist, and believed that *everything* – thoughts, even God – was simply matter in motion, knocking around like billiard balls in an unbroken chain of cause and effect. Having read Euclid's *Elements* he became, as Aubrey observed, 'in love with geometry', so much so 'that he was wont to draw lines on his thigh and on the sheets, abed'. Moving swiftly on from Hobbes's night-time exploits, the point is that he was captivated by the deductive method. His abiding desire was to ground all knowledge on it, and in doing so unfurl one systematic science.

At various points in his life, however, political reality intruded upon Hobbes's scientific preoccupations and inspired from his pen some of the most unanswerable as well as outrageous claims about civic life. In the late 1630s objections began to be raised to the absoluteness of Charles I's rule, flaunted most flagrantly when he tried to raise the 'Ship Money' tax without the consent of Parliament in 1637. Hobbes, a devoted Royalist, joined the fray by writing *The Elements of Law*, a defence of absolute sovereignty, indeed a proclamation that unless sovereignty was absolute it was no sovereignty at all. Fearing that what he had written would endanger his life in the brewing rebellion, Hobbes fled to Paris in 1640, and from there watched with horror as the King was forced to raise his royal standard at Nottingham in 1642 and formally declare war on Parliament. What followed was an astonishing episode in English history, friends and family were divided and killed, and in 1649 the revolutionaries chopped off the head of the King.

One cannot underestimate how this all seared into Hobbes's mind. It tormented him personally, as when, for example, as he tells us in his verse autobiography, he lost his friend Sidney Godolphin, 'Soldier Belov'd', in a skirmish in 1643, saddling him with 'A weighty Lasting Grief'. It is this traumatic context which makes sense of the extremity of Hobbes's political thought. The pain that was hewn in the English Civil War explains why Hobbes was so convinced that revolution is bad and government good, that however irritating and uncomfortable, law is better than anarchy. That often romanticized condition of nature Hobbes saw with his own eyes was nothing more elevated than a war of all against all, where not principles but lives were squashed underfoot. This is where his instruction comes from that when we find ourselves complaining about politicians, we should call to mind the dreadful alternative, and hush now.

Much as it wounded him, however, the rebels were winning. England's protection now lay with them, and it was this fact which formed the ultimate backdrop for *Leviathan*. Although it is saturated with his Royalist and anti-revolutionary sensibilities, and retains much of the architecture of his previous political writing, it was written as the tide was turning in Cromwell's favour and published in 1651. It concludes with a heavy-hearted explanation to himself as much as to his monarchist friends of why it was reasonable for them to switch allegiance to their old foes, indeed why they should. Besides, Hobbes was tired of self-imposed exile in France and wanted to go home. *Leviathan*, however, was no simply pragmatic publication: it would help him make peace with the new order, certainly, but peace, as we shall see, is the supreme moral good, and worth sacrificing pride and even principle for.

While it eased his passage back to England, *Leviathan* caused Hobbes grief for much of the rest of his life. Fulminating feverishly as he does in the book against religious 'enthusiasts' and clerics of all habits (Anglican, Presbyterian, Catholic), as well as lawyers and the universities, and spouting some wildly unorthodox moral and religious opinions, Hobbes was deemed a menacing heretic. Indeed, for decades to come after his death in 1679, to be called a 'Hobbist' was to be assaulted by one of the most unpleasant insults imaginable.

Let me see what I can do to rehabilitate him, or rather to reveal the insights that he possessed despite – and sometimes because of – the darkness, and the sparks that they might ignite in our albeit very different twenty-first-century minds. While Hobbes wrote many works, the lessons of this book are drawn exclusively from *Leviathan*, his English masterpiece. But first, a warning about his prose: while much of the archaic spelling and typography has been evened out to make it easier to read, it can still, like his arguments, be intimidating. Have faith, however. Marked not only by his love for deductive reasoning, it is also rich with wit and metaphor. There's gold, if you dig, and in the first nugget we learn of perhaps our greatest enemy: fear.

# 1

# ON LIVING
# IN FEAR

..........

Fear is a fact of life, but it can suffocate us, snaking its
way into our every thought if we are not careful – will
I be attacked? Will I lose my job? Will my child fall out
of that tree? Do people hate me? Am I any good at all?
Fear can make us withdraw from the world or lash out
at it, but either way, if left to fester, it is a desperately
unproductive emotion and renders us incapable of
concentrating on anything else. Hobbes's extraordinary
contribution is to make us reflect on just how paralysing
and introverting this emotion can be, and how the State
plays a crucial role in releasing us from it. He asks us to
imagine 'the natural condition of mankind' – what our
lives would be like without the State to protect us from
the invasions of our fellow human beings. Stripping
away all the artifice that civilizes us, he forces us to take
a clear-eyed look at ourselves. It is here, gazing uneasily
into the mirror, that we discover both the inevitability as
well as the horror of mutual fear.

He reasoned his way to this conclusion by employ-
ing the deductive method of which he was so fond,

and by beginning with the fundamental truth of human equality:

> NATURE has made men so equal in the faculties of body and mind as that, though there be found one man sometimes manifestly stronger in body, or of quicker mind than another, yet when all is reckoned together the difference between man and man is not so considerable, as that one man can thereupon claim to himself any benefit, to which another may not pretend as well as he. For as to the strength of body, the weakest has strength enough to kill the strongest, either by secret machination, or by confederacy with others that are in the same danger with himself.
>
> And as to the faculties of the mind . . . I find yet a greater equality amongst men, than that of strength. For prudence is but experience; which equal time equally bestows on all men in those things they equally apply themselves unto. That which may perhaps make such equality incredible, is but a vain conceit of one's own wisdom, which almost all men think they have in a greater degree than the vulgar; that is, than all men but themselves, and a few others, whom by fame, or for concurring with themselves, they approve. For such is the nature of men, that howsoever they may acknowledge many others to be more witty, or more eloquent, or more learned,

yet they will hardly believe there be many so wise as themselves: for they see their own wit at hand, and other men's at a distance. But this proves rather that men are in that point equal, than unequal. For there is not ordinarily a greater sign of the equal distribution of anything, than that every man is contented with his share.

(Leviathan, chapter 13)

Although our individual bodies might be weaker than those of others, we can make up for this with guile and strength in numbers. When it comes to the mind, the differences between us are even more negligible. While a few are capable of the heights of reason, most of us have only experience as our guide, and in this we are very much alike. All of us for example have put our fingers near the fire, and know not to venture closer. All of us have confided in people who have then betrayed our trust, and made us wary of confiding as a result.

Hobbes admits that this equality might come as a shock to us. We tend to think of ourselves as having so much more understanding than other people. But this is just a trick of perspective. The first-person knowledge we have of our thoughts gives us the illusion of superior insight. Insofar as our ideas provide our only access to the world, they seem to us to tell the truth, to represent the reality of things. Our opinions are completely present to us and therefore feel more substantial than the far-off observations of others, muffled as they are through language and vain, deaf ears. Only the famous, or those who agree with us, as Hobbes observes with characteristic wryness, seem to match up to our brilliance.

This overinflated sense of our own merit is nothing other than pride – that sin which is as deep in human nature as it is mistaken. We are in reality pretty much alike in capacity, and it is because of this basic similarity that Hobbes comes to his famous determination that the natural condition of man is a condition of war:

> From this equality of ability arises equality of hope in the attaining of our ends. And therefore if any two men desire the same thing, which nevertheless they cannot both enjoy, they become enemies; and in the way to their end (which is principally their own conservation, and sometimes their delectation only) endeavour to destroy or subdue one another. And from hence it comes to pass that where an invader has no more to fear than another man's single power, if one plant, sow, build, or possess a convenient seat, others may probably be expected to come prepared with forces united to dispossess and deprive him, not only of the fruit of his labour, but also of his life or liberty. And the invader again is in the like danger of another.
>
> And from this diffidence of one another, there is no way for any man to secure himself so reasonable

as anticipation; that is, by force, or wiles, to master the persons of all men he can so long till he see no other power great enough to endanger him: and this is no more than his own conservation requires, and is generally allowed. Also, because there be some that, taking pleasure in contemplating their own power in the acts of conquest, which they pursue farther than their security requires; if others, that otherwise would be glad to be at ease within modest bounds, should not by invasion increase their power, they would not be able, long time, by standing only on their defence, to subsist. And by consequence, such augmentation of dominion over men being necessary to a man's conservation, it ought to be allowed him.

Again, men have no pleasure (but on the contrary a great deal of grief) in keeping company where there is no power able to overawe them all. For every man looks that his companion should value him at the same rate he sets upon himself, and upon all signs of contempt, or undervaluing, naturally endeavours, as far as he dares (which amongst them that have no common power to keep them in quiet, is far enough to make them destroy each other), to extort a greater value from his contemners, by damage; and from others, by the example.

So that in the nature of man, we find three principal causes of quarrel. First, competition; secondly, diffidence; thirdly, glory.

> The first, makes men invade for gain; the second, for safety; and the third, for reputation. The first use violence, to make themselves masters of other men's persons, wives, children, and cattle; the second, to defend them; the third, for trifles, as a word, a smile, a different opinion, and any other sign of undervalue, either direct in their persons or by reflection in their kindred, their friends, their nation, their profession, or their name.
>
> (*Leviathan*, chapter 13)

In Hobbes's rational reconstruction of what would happen if individuals were left entirely free and unchecked, they end up afraid and destructive of each other. Each of us has to survive, and wants the food or the possessions or the lover that someone else has; and, because the other person is no stronger than we are, we quite reasonably want to take what they have worked for. Being equal, then, we are all equally in danger of trespasses from each other. There are those of an especially anxious disposition who feel overwhelmed by the conviction that their neighbour is going to come for them at any moment, and so they mount a pre-emptive strike in an attempt to crush them before they themselves are crushed (haven't we all, in paranoid and pressured moments, imagined that a colleague, or even a friend, wants to undermine us, and struck out, creating a 'situation' that need never have been?). And then there are the vainglorious, who attack others not so much for the necessities of life but rather because they relish the subjugation and servility of others, and who fly into conquering violence when they feel disrespected or undervalued by a mere sigh or an over-long stare.

It appears, therefore, that Hobbes's state of nature is not the bland, game-theoretical clash of equally acquisitive individuals that is often supposed. Rather, it is a complex war set in motion by the needs of life and a kaleidoscope of desires that pattern human interaction.

This picture of a fraught environment which none of us wanted or enjoys but which has nonetheless been created by us is surely familiar – both at work and at home. I might be a modest person, content with just enough, but I am forced by the logic of competition and finite resources to enter the fray. I might be a generous person, genuinely delighted with the success of others, but I find myself envied and drawn reluctantly into battle, cowed by hurt, and internalizing the jealousy I did not invite. We all know too well the feeling that we did not ask for this and yet here we are, struggling for example in an office or a friendship in a way that is making everyone involved feel bad. We each believe that we began in innocence but have been infected by bitter-ness and sucked into suspicion. People come, moreover, in all shades of personalities, but the fact that there are some with domineering and malicious intent pulls us all, even those of us who prefer to run away, somehow into the game.

The state of nature is not just a thought experiment to explain the benefits of government, but it is a description of the dynamic of conflict which seeps more or less obviously into everyday experience. As Hobbes says, war consists not only in battle but also in the threat of it, in the intimidating, sulking glower of those who seem determined to be our antagonists. It is like the weather, foul not only when the rain whips and the thunder booms but also when the clouds are filled with menace. Combat need not be under way to disrupt us; the icy fingers of a cold war can unsettle us just as well, as anyone living in the second half of the twentieth century, or indeed probably any wife or husband *ever*, can attest.

For those readers of Hobbes who do not want to believe in his pessimistic portrait of unfettered human nature, he provides some real examples: lawless barbarians running through the forests of the new world; or nations themselves continually poised against each other in actual or potential war, equipped to the hilt with espionage and arms; or, most resonantly, his readers themselves who had been, and still were to an extent, pitted brother against brother in England's Civil War. Even putting these extremities aside, in normal life, Hobbes challenges his readers, why, if they so trust their fellow man, do they lock their doors?

It may seem strange to some man, that has not well weighed these things, that Nature should thus dissociate and render men apt to invade and destroy one another: and he may therefore, not trusting to this inference, made from the passions, desire perhaps to have the same confirmed by experience. Let him therefore consider with himself: when taking a journey, he arms himself and seeks to go well accompanied; when going to sleep, he locks his doors; when even in his house he locks his chests; and this when he knows there be laws and public officers, armed, to revenge all injuries [that] shall be done [to] him; what opinion he has of his fellow subjects, when he rides armed; of his fellow citizens, when he locks his doors; and of his children, and servants, when he locks his chests. Does he not there as much accuse mankind by his actions as I do by my words? But neither of us accuse[s] man's nature in it. The desires, and other passions of man, are in themselves no sin. No more are the actions, that proceed from those passions, till they know a law that forbids them; which till laws be made they cannot know, nor can any law be made till they have agreed upon the person that shall make it.

It may peradventure be thought, there was never such a time, nor condition of war as this; and I believe it was never generally so, over all the world: but there are many places where they live so now. For the savage people in many places of America, except the government of small families, the concord whereof depends on natural lust, have no government at all; and live at this day in that brutish manner, as I said before. Howsoever, it may be perceived what manner of life there would be, where there were no common power to fear, by the manner of life which men that have formerly lived under a peaceful government, use to degenerate into a civil war.

But though there had never been any time, wherein particular men were in a condition of war one against another; yet in all times kings, and persons of sovereign authority, because of their independency, are in continual jealousies, and in the state and posture of gladiators; having their weapons pointing, and their eyes fixed on one another; that is, their forts, garrisons, and guns upon the frontiers of their kingdoms, and continual spies upon their neighbours, which is a posture of war.

(*Leviathan*, chapter 13)

Fear, then, and mutual mistrust lurk even under the carapace of law and, uncontained, threaten to undo us entirely. It is not just that left to our own devices we might injure one another, but that in such a state of uncertainty we must keep our eyes fixed on the mundane and cannot get on with scaling the heights of human possibility. Forever preoccupied with our safety, we have neither time nor head space to realize our full potential, as Hobbes makes clear in that most famous (and often misunderstood) aria in *Leviathan*:

> Whatsoever therefore is consequent to a time of war, where every man is enemy to every man, the same consequent to the time, wherein men live without other security than what their own strength, and their own invention shall furnish them withal. In such condition, there is no place for industry; because the fruit thereof is uncertain: and consequently no culture of the earth; no navigation, nor use of the commodities that may be imported by sea; no commodious building; no instruments of moving and removing such things as require much force; no knowledge of the face of the earth; no account of time; no arts; no letters; no society; and which is worst of all, continual fear, and danger of violent death; and the life of man, solitary, poor, nasty, brutish, and short.
>
> (*Leviathan*, chapter 13)

It is not *men*, then, who are intrinsically nasty, brutish and short (Aubrey reports that Hobbes was a good six foot), but their *lives*, when they are unprotected. Men and indeed women come in a multiplicity of characters (and, I might say, sizes), many of them kind and open-hearted. They are made wary of each other when the organizations to which they belong do not make them feel secure. A world without security is not only a frightening but a fruitless place, and turns its inhabitants into beasts in spite of all their better intentions and the panoply of passions that want to burst from their breasts, such as joy, benevolence, magnanimity, fortitude, liberality, love, curiosity, admiration and laughter, to name but a few of Hobbes's examples. What Hobbes's philosophy offers is a safe space where these equally natural seeds in human beings might flourish, where we might be emancipated from fear and therefore receive the gift not only of life, but of the opportunity to thrive.

Just before we move into the sun, however, it is worth recognizing the thread of fear which is an irrevocable part of all relationships at some point in their trajectory. Recalling Hobbes's principle of equality, we should seek the strength to overcome that most debilitating of emotions, as well as own up to any part that we played in its generation.

# 2

# ON LIVING
# WITHOUT FEAR

..........

In what has seemed to many too outrageous a paradox, Hobbes says that the only way in which you can free yourself from the fear of your fellow human beings, is by creating a monster so terrifying that none of them would dare attack you for fear of what the monster might do to them. This is the monster of the State – in our day the nuclear warheads that point at other States to deter them from attacking us, the policemen on the streets who make that fellow who wants my purse think better of it. Leaving aside for the moment the question of what happens if the monster were to turn on YOU, Hobbes's thought is that unless it is spectacularly, incomparably more powerful than ordinary men, it will not be able to contain them, some of whom, we remember, are fatally proud. With massively exaggerated views of their own importance, these idiots would carry on attacking people regardless, as well as rise up against any putative leader trying to lord it over them, thereby hurling the country into precisely the sort of civil war the monster is supposed to prevent.

This idea that politics is fundamentally a mechanism to subdue pride has a long history. It was pride which led Adam to rebel against God and which brought evil into the world, infecting the postlapsarian psyche ever since. Although as we shall see Hobbes is extremely sceptical about the claims of religion, he nonetheless realizes and appropriates the huge power that the Bible exerts over his readers, as well as subscribing to its grim assessment of the fallen nature of man. Just as St Augustine had stated in the *City of God* that the almighty power of Rome was necessary to keep a lid on men's *libido dominandi* (lust for domination) and prevent it boiling over into all-out carnage, so Hobbes declared that government had to be strong in order to subdue men who think misguidedly that they know better than anyone else and are therefore prone to sedition and disorder. Politics, itself a kind of pride whereby some men dominate others, emerges from this angle as a necessary evil which keeps in check the pride of men. This is why Hobbes chooses as his metaphor for the State that great sea beast Leviathan who, as Scripture says, is 'King of all the children of pride'.

Hobbes's account of how and why we make the State is as follows. Each of us has a natural right to use whatever power we have to preserve ourselves, even – given that the condition of nature is a condition of war – to kill another person if we think that will save us. Since it is impossible to be safe in such a situation, people work out that the fundamental principle which ought to govern their lives is to seek peace. The only way to do this is if everybody agrees to lay down their right to all things so that just as I may no longer attack you, you may no longer attack me, and we give to ourselves only as much liberty as we are happy for others to possess. The problem in the condition of nature is that there is no good reason for any of us to refrain from attacking others because we cannot be sure – indeed we would be foolish to think – that others will not attack us. Instead, they are likely to dispossess and destroy us all the quicker. The only way to force people not to violate each other is to erect a body so awesome that it will petrify them into compliance. They therefore agree to give their powers up to a sovereign and let him or her represent them, and in doing so, they create the body of the State – an agglomeration of all the power of all the people: a body with precisely the kind of overwhelming power that we have been looking for. In Hobbes's grand announcement:

The only way to erect such a common power, as may be able to defend them from the invasion of foreigners, and the injuries of one another, and thereby to secure them in such sort, as that by their own industry, and by the fruits of the earth, they may nourish themselves and live contentedly; is to confer all their power and strength upon one man, or upon one assembly of men, that may reduce all their wills, by plurality of voices, unto one will: which is as much as to say, to appoint one man, or assembly of men, to bear their person; and every one to own and acknowledge himself to be author of whatsoever he that so bears their person shall act, or cause to be acted, in those things which concern the common peace and safety; and therein to submit their wills, every one to his will, and their judgements to his judgement. This is more than consent, or concord; it is a real unity of them all, in one and the same person, made by covenant of every man with every man, in such manner, as if every man should say to every man: *I authorise and give up my right of governing myself to this man, or to this assembly of men, on this condition; that thou give up, thy right to him, and authorise all his actions in like manner.* This done, the multitude so united in one person is called a COMMONWEALTH; in Latin, CIVITAS. This is the generation of that great LEVIATHAN, or rather (to speak more reverently) of that mortal god to which we owe, under the immortal God, our peace and defence. For by this authority, given him by every particular man in the Commonwealth, he has the use of so much power and strength conferred on him that, by terror thereof, he is enabled to conform the wills of them all, to peace at home, and mutual aid against their enemies abroad. And in him consists the essence

26

of the Commonwealth; which (to define it) is: one person, of whose acts a great multitude, by mutual covenants one with another, have made themselves every one the author, to the end he may use the strength and means of them all, as he shall think expedient, for their peace and common defence.

And he that carries this person is called sovereign, and said to have sovereign power; and every one besides, his subject.

(*Leviathan*, chapter 17)

If this dense description of the State is hard to grasp, the frontispiece of *Leviathan* makes plain just what it should look like. A giant sovereign is pictured towering over the country, and his body is made up of hundreds of tiny subjects. This is the State, its people only unified into one body when it has a sovereign to bear its person. It cannot exist without a representative, and is therefore sometimes hard to distinguish from that omnipotent sovereign.

As unlikely as it may seem, our only hope is to construct this mortal god. The sovereign, like the Leviathan he animates, has to dazzle and blind like the sun. He must have absolute and unaccountable power if he is to pull off this trick of peace. The history of absolute leaders such as Stalin and Pol Pot has pressed home what happens when the mortal god trains his guns against his people and clearly this is a heinous element of Hobbes's thinking. But while we rightly baulk at the extremity of his position, it is worth noting that for Hobbes these would be far from ideal leaders. Preferably, he advises princes, they should rule by clear laws that serve the interests of the people, and there should be equality before the law irrespective of wealth and status. His point though is that even if a government is not perfect, indeed is quite iniquitous, it is bound in most cases to be better than no government at all. Remember that he was writing in the wreckage of civil strife, which brought home the benefits rather than the costs of a strong State in a way that is hard to appreciate if we have not suffered something similar.

We might get a flash of the wisdom of Hobbes if we consider the removal of the governments in Afghanistan and even Iraq in 2001 and 2003 respectively. It is still not obvious (and it certainly was not obvious at the time) whether the bloodletting and chaos that followed the foreign interventions have been preferable for the majority of the people trying to live in those places. And when, following the disarray of Yeltsin's freer rule, many Russians voted for a return to the strong government of the autocrat Putin, they seemed to be proving Hobbes's point. Even if we look to our own doorsteps, to the London riots of 2011, we can see not only that a kind of Hobbesian disorder (and a sense of disenfranchisement and alienation) does indeed simmer very close to the surface of supposedly civilized nations, but that when it boils over even the usually liberal commentariat call for the police to crack down, rather than stand impotently and lawfully by. Usually shielded from war by the very thing we like to censure, we do not always see as clearly as Hobbes could see the value of the State.

Authority by its very nature can be uncomfortable. None of us likes being ordered to do anything, especially if we'd rather be doing the opposite. What Hobbes prompts us to do is take a few steps back from the government that we loathe, for its intrusions, injustices and cock-ups, and imagine the alternative. Through the rule of law, we are able most days to walk down the road without being mugged, to sleep in our homes without being burgled, to remonstrate without being killed. Fencing us off from the unwelcome and unpredictable incursions of others, and freeing us from the paralysing fear that poisons this predicament, the State brings not only peace, and peace of mind, but also room to expand ourselves, to paint, to party, to prosper. Far from championing fear as an instrument of control, Hobbes's overriding concern is to work out how we can most effectively escape this crippling emotion. According to him it is only the short-sighted and the criminal who hate and fear the government; those who have considered life without it find that these negative sentiments are transformed into a grudging appreciation.

Moreover, although Hobbes is often and with good reason reviled for the way in which he seems to divest us as individuals of all autonomy, subsuming us under the totalizing power of the State, it is important to remark the extent to which we can find in Hobbes the albeit faint contours of modern representative democracy. He believes that a social contract is necessary to legitimate the government. We are not forced to obey it; we choose to. Indeed, we are, according to Hobbes, the authors of its actions. We are the State.

Indeed, in an exhilarating depiction of our agency, Hobbes compares us to God. Just as he created the world, so we create our own salvation in the form of the artificial person of the State:

> NATURE (the art whereby God has made and governs the world) is by the art of man, as in many other things, so in this also imitated, that it can make an artificial animal. For seeing life is but a motion of limbs, the beginning whereof is in some principal part within; why may we not say that all automata (engines that move themselves by springs and wheels as does a watch) have an artificial life? For what is the heart, but a spring; and the nerves, but so many strings; and the joints, but so many wheels, giving motion to the whole body, such as was intended by the Artificer? Art goes yet further, imitating that rational and most excellent

work of Nature, man. For by art is created that great LEVIATHAN called a COMMONWEALTH, or STATE. . ., which is but an artificial man; though of greater stature and strength than the natural, for whose protection and defence it was intended; and in which the sovereignty is an artificial soul, as giving life and motion to the whole body; the magistrates and other officers of judicature and execution, artificial joints; reward and punishment (by which fastened to the seat of the sovereignty, every joint and member is moved to perform his duty) are the nerves, that do the same in the body natural; the wealth and riches of all the particular members are the strength; *salus populi* (the people's safety) its business; counsellors, by whom all things needful for it to know are suggested unto it, are the memory; equity and laws, an artificial reason and will; concord, health; sedition, sickness; and civil war, death. Lastly, the pacts and covenants, by which the parts of this body politic were at first made, set together, and united, resemble that fiat, or the *Let us make man*, pronounced by God in the Creation.

(*Leviathan*, Introduction)

There is one limit to the obedience we owe this towering figure: we may resist it if it attacks our liberty – the protection of which is the basic purpose of the State, and the subject of the next chapter.

# 3

# ON BEING FREE

..........

Pouring scorn on the clamour for human rights, Hobbes makes a statement that has become a bulwark of Western political discourse ever since those planes blasted into the World Trade Center on September 11th 2001: we have to make a trade-off between rights and security that is easy for us to forget in times of peace. We want the right to privacy, to use search engines and send emails free from the invasive eyes of big brother. When the police cart us off, we want the right to know what it is that we are charged with having done wrong, and then to be judged in public by a jury of our peers. But in recent years governments in shades of red and blue alike have eroded these rights, assuring us that if we've done nothing wrong then we have nothing to fear (and anyway it's 'them' not 'us' they have in their sights), insisting that sometimes rights have to be sacrificed in order to keep us safe. My stomach twists at this sleight of hand, and I know, against Hobbes, that I never want the government to be unbridled.

But, just as I know that security ought not to come at any price, I must admit that it has to come at some price. This is the lesson that liberalism has to confront, and it was Hobbes who laid it down in its starkest form. If we each had the right to do whatever we pleased, we would end up killing each other, says Hobbes, and so we must embrace our constraints. We ought to relish our submission, conscious that we perform it in exchange for our lives. This apparent move against liberty is part of the way in which, as we will see, Hobbes turns the entire edifice of our value structure on its head. Here we find him unpacking the nice-sounding idea of human rights as something not only to be feared rather than coveted, but moreover as a complete fiction. If I have unlimited right and so do you, then it comes to nothing in the end. It cancels itself out, so that no one has any power to do anything at all, as we each cower behind barred doors.

Hobbes's critique of empty and untrammelled rights speaks particularly powerfully to us now, not only as particular rights claims multiply riotously, so that everyone seems to be asserting all manner of far-fetched entitlements such as the right to write venomous anonymous comments on the Internet, but also as governments and corporations trumpet rights which they have no hope – or indeed perhaps, no intention – of enforcing. It is not just that it is useless to talk, for example, about the rights to healthcare, education and non-discrimination, if hospitals, schools and inequality are as a matter of fact getting worse, but it is an insult to those struggling with these facts. What is more, the edifying language of rights can be used as a sop by those in power to shirk their practical duties and cover up the desolate reality.

Having explained why we have to give up our rights (which anyway come to no more than hot air), Hobbes then performs a characteristically daring act of redefinition: the security that is delivered by the apparent renunciation of one's freedom when we enter the State is nothing other than – wait for it – freedom properly understood! Expropriating the rightly beloved term away from mistaken and dangerous speakers, he tells us what it really means. In Hobbes's materialist universe, it should be applied only to bodies, and it signifies the absence of external impediments to motion. Just as a stream, then, is free if it is not stopped by a dam, so a person is free if she or he is not restrained by chains or a prison gate. This freedom to move as one wants is freedom proper.

And unlike the self-defeating plenitude of natural right, this physical liberty is not nothing. The freedom from the interference of others enables one to relax, to stretch out into life. As Hobbes elaborates, what we need is not simply the power to govern our own bodies, but also to

> enjoy air, water, motion, ways to go from place to
> place; and all things else without which a man cannot
> live, or not live well.
>
> (*Leviathan*, chapter 15)

Note here Hobbes's explicit echoing of Aristotle's vaulting ambition for civilization: a place where we can not only live but live well. Far from losing liberty in a strong State, we win it there. That is the point of the State.

By the same token, when our corporeal liberty is infringed by the government we have the right to defend ourselves and make alternative arrangements for our protection. We do not therefore write a totally blank cheque to Leviathan. We have the right to fight back if it extends its claws on us. As Hobbes explains, we only agree to obey the sovereign in the first place because we want him to protect us, and it would thus be inconceivable for us to agree to let that same sovereign attack us. It would be insane. The social contract must accordingly leave us with the right of individual resistance.

> Whensoever a man transfers his right, or renounces
> it, it is either in consideration of some right recipro-
> cally transferred to himself, or for some other good
> he hopes for thereby. For it is a voluntary act: and of
> the voluntary acts of every man, the object is some

good to himself. And therefore there be some rights which no man can be understood by any words, or other signs, to have abandoned or transferred. As first a man cannot lay down the right of resisting them that assault him by force to take away his life, because he cannot be understood to aim thereby at any good to himself. The same may be said of wounds, and chains, and imprisonment; both because there is no benefit consequent to such patience; as there is to the patience of suffering another to be wounded, or imprisoned: as also because a man cannot tell when he sees men proceed against him by violence whether they intend his death or not. And lastly the motive, and end for which this renouncing and trans- ferring of right is introduced, is nothing else but the security of a man's person, in his life, and in the means of so preserving life, as not to be weary of it. And therefore if a man by words, or other signs, seem to despoil himself of the end for which those signs were intended, he is not to be understood as if he meant it, or that it was his will, but that he was ignorant of how such words and actions were to be interpreted.

(*Leviathan*, chapter 14)

Even if we have committed wicked crimes, if the sovereign comes for our liberty, we may, indeed we must, counter-attack. Likewise, if the sovereign can no longer protect our liberty, then our obligation to him is dissolved:

> The obligation of subjects to the sovereign is understood to last as long, and no longer, than the power lasts by which he is able to protect them. For the right men have by nature to protect themselves, when none else can protect them, can by no covenant be relinquished. The sovereignty is the soul of the Commonwealth; which, once departed from the body, the members do no more receive their motion from it. The end of obedience is protection; which, wheresoever a man sees it, either in his own, or in another's sword, nature applies his obedience to it, and his endeavour to maintain it. And though sovereignty, in the intention of them that make it, be immortal; yet is it in its own nature, not only subject to violent death by foreign war, but also through the ignorance and passions of men it has in it, from the very institution, many seeds of a natural mortality, by intestine discord.
>
> If a subject be taken prisoner in war, or his person, or his means of life be within the guards of the enemy, and has his life and corporal liberty given him, on condition to be subject to the victor, he has liberty to accept the condition; and, having accepted it, is the subject of him that took him; because he had no other way to preserve himself. The case is

> the same, if he be detained on the same terms, in
> a foreign country. But if a man be held in prison, or
> bonds, or is not trusted with the liberty of his body;
> he cannot be understood to be bound by covenant to
> subjection; and therefore may, if he can, make his
> escape by any means whatsoever.
>
> (*Leviathan*, chapter 21)

There it is, the core of politics: 'the end of obedience is protection', and when we are no longer protected we are no longer bound to obey. Remember that the Leviathan is a *mortal* god, animated only by its rulers who are themselves human. Like all humans, they can be killed, either by a foreign conqueror or indeed by their own people. And this, of course, is precisely what happened in England in 1649, when the Parliamentarians executed Charles I. It pained Hobbes to say it, but this rendered that particular man unambiguously incapable of keeping his subjects safe. This is why, late in 1650, when he was dashing to finish *Leviathan* and Cromwell's ascendancy was pretty clear, he added 'A Review, and Conclusion' to that intensely Royalist tract which inveighs against rebels right up until they win:

> And because I find by diverse English books lately
> printed, that the civil wars have not yet suffi-
> ciently taught men, in what point of time it is that

a subject becomes obliged to the conqueror; nor what is conquest; nor how it comes about that it obliges men to obey his laws: therefore for further satisfaction of men therein, I say, the point of time wherein a man becomes subject to a conqueror is that point wherein, having liberty to submit to him, he consents, either by express words, or by other sufficient sign, to be his subject. When it is that a man has the liberty to submit . . . it is then, when the means of his life is within the guards and garrisons of the enemy; for it is then, that he has no longer protection from him, but is protected by the adverse party for his contribution.

(*Leviathan*, A Review, and Conclusion)

Liberty, then, properly understood, constitutes both the purpose *and the limit* of obligation, and we are obliged to whomever sets us free.

There is something very lonely in this lesson. There is no scope for collective action, only atomised individuals struggling with the noose, with no expectation of anyone coming to their aid. And the fact that they tie themselves to whomever it is that happens to look after them evokes the looseness of the ties that bind us to one another. It is a solitary figure who stares at his or her routed comrades and knows it will be safer to change sides. The strains of the 'Marseillaise' are not very audible for the person resisting on the scaffold.

Prosaically now, when we (or our children) start at school or university, we are quick to establish new and useful alliances. When we change jobs, our allegiances switch almost automatically. We are joined to friends, to institutions and even to our nation with bonds which sometimes seem to hold us so tightly that we feel that we are flying, but which often turn out to be contingent on fair weather. Even family, where the connections are indelible, can feel elusive. Hobbes reminds us of the pleasure as well as the ache of the fact of our isolation.

# 4

# ON FEELING FREE

..........

Hobbes's insistence that he has delivered the proper definition of liberty has a pugnacious, dialogical edge to it because he is trying to disprove a rival definition which he thinks is not only wrong but, more pertinently, partly to blame for the Civil War. That is to say, he developed his account of liberty in *Leviathan* as a response to what has become known as the republican view – a theory about freedom and slavery marshalled by Parliamentarians against the King in the 1640s, and which, as we will see, has much merit in it. This is a story I have learned not from Hobbes directly, but from the historian Quentin Skinner. He has shown that one can only fully understand the contours of Hobbes's twisting views on liberty if one sees them as polemical interventions in a political battle. This is therefore not simply a lesson about what it means to be free, but also about the methodology of the history of ideas: the meanings of canonical texts can be illuminated if one situates them in the contexts which originally urged pen to paper. Hobbes's words can speak to us, but do so more authentically, and often more richly, if we work out what they meant to him.

What infuriated Hobbes was a view espoused in antiquity, especially in the Roman republic, and then renovated in the English Revolution, that one cannot be free if one is dependent on the goodwill of someone else. A free man, or *liber homo*, is, as the *Digest* of Roman Law puts it, is under his own power, rather than that of a master. If someone has the power arbitrarily to intervene in our lives, even if they do not actually intervene, then we are slaves. Even if they permit us complete freedom of action, this freedom is a matter of privilege, and not of right. It is something that we have been granted but that can be taken away at any point, rather than something that we can enjoy with certainty. This is why, the argument goes, we are slaves under an absolute monarch, and can only be free if we live in what republican theorists call a 'free State' – a self-governing republic, or at least a constitutional monarchy governed by the rule of law, in which not only are we as citizens free from arbitrary power, but which itself is run according to the will of all (rather than the private will of the monarch), and is therefore free and happy.

Hobbes is enraged by the books which have spread this poison. It has worked people up into a frenzy, making them believe that they can only profit in a 'free State', that they are slaves under a king, and must therefore slay him, provided for the sake of their deluded consciences they rename him a tyrant – a ludicrous name according to Hobbes, signifying simply a monarch disliked. The ancient 'democraticall writers', who Hobbes says are the sources for this view, are like a rabid dog that has bitten the Stuarts. It would have been better, sighs Hobbes (a grandmaster of the Renaissance), never to have learned Latin or Greek, the price of which has been nothing less than the blood of Englishmen.

It is this agonized context which makes sense of Hobbes's protest that he knows the *proper* meaning of liberty. This is why he is so emphatic that freedom can only be predicated of bodies. Sharpening his quill, he counter-attacks the idea that a man is unfree if he moves about at the discretion of someone else, with the cool observation that a man free to move about as he wants is plainly free. It does not matter a jot to the experience of freedom what kind of government or authority one lives under. Personal freedom is all the same, wherever you are lucky enough to enjoy it, and it is therefore entirely unconnected to political freedom – which is itself a nonsense. All States are as free as each other, and anyway, it isn't anything to crow about, being free like this – it just means that each State is in the same miserable and embattled predicament that people are in when they have unlimited right in the condition of nature. One can almost see Hobbes jumping up and down, as he points out the absurdity of the republicans' position. Can they see any physical obstacles blocking their way? No! They are free. It is 'very absurd', therefore, 'for men to clamour as they do for the liberty they so manifestly enjoy'.

LIBERTY, or freedom, signifies (properly) the absence of opposition (by opposition, I mean external impediments of motion); and may be applied no less to irrational and inanimate creatures than to rational. For whatsoever is so tied, or environed, as it cannot move but within a certain space, which space is determined by the opposition of some external body, we say it has not liberty to go further. And so of all living creatures, whilst they are imprisoned, or restrained with walls or chains; and of the water whilst it is kept in by banks, or vessels, that otherwise would spread itself into a larger space; we use to say they are not at liberty to move in such manner, as without those external impediments they would. But when the impediment of motion is in the constitution of the thing itself, we use not to say it wants the liberty, but the power, to move; as when a stone lies still, or a man is fastened to his bed by sickness.

And according to this proper, and generally received meaning of the word, a free-man is he that, in those things which by his strength and wit he is able to do, is not hindered to do what he has a will to. But when the words free and liberty are applied to anything but bodies, they are abused ... Lastly, from the use of the words free will, no liberty can be inferred of the will, desire, or inclination, but the liberty of the man; which consists in this, that he finds no stop in doing what he has the will, desire, or inclination to do . . .

The liberty, whereof there is so frequent and honourable mention in the histories and philosophy of the ancient Greeks and Romans, and in the writings and discourse of those that from them have received all their learning in the politics, is not the liberty of particular men; but the liberty of the Commonwealth: which is the same with that which every man then should have, if there were no civil laws nor Commonwealth at all. And the effects of it also be the same. For as amongst masterless men, there is perpetual war of every man against his neighbour; no inheritance to transmit to the son, nor to expect from the father; no propriety of goods or lands; no security; but a full and absolute liberty in every particular man: so in states and Commonwealths not dependent on one another, every Commonwealth (not every man) has an absolute liberty to do what it shall judge (that is to say, what that man or assembly that represents it shall judge) most conducing to their benefit. But withal, they live in the condition of a perpetual war, and upon the confines of battle, with their frontiers armed, and cannons planted against their neighbours round about. The Athenians and Romans were free; that is, free Commonwealths: not that any particular men had the liberty to resist their own representative; but that their representative had the liberty to resist, or invade, other people. There is written on the turrets of the city of Lucca in great characters at this day, the word LIBERTAS; yet no man can thence infer that a particular man has more liberty, or immunity from the service of the Commonwealth there, than in Constantinople. Whether a Commonwealth be monarchical, or popular, the freedom is still the same.

But it is an easy thing for men to be deceived by the specious name of liberty . . .

(*Leviathan*, chapter 21)

Later on, when Hobbes is enumerating 'those things that weaken, or tend to the dissolution of a commonwealth', he evinces just what harm can be caused by the deceptive and constitutive power of names:

And as to rebellion in particular against monarchy; one of the most frequent causes of it is the reading of the books of policy and histories of the ancient Greeks and Romans; from which young men, and all others that are unprovided of the antidote of solid reason, receiving a strong and delightful impression of the great exploits of war, achieved by the conductors of their armies, receive withal a pleasing idea of all they have done besides; and imagine their great prosperity, not to have proceeded from the emulation of particular men, but from the virtue of their popular form of government not considering the frequent seditions and civil wars produced by the imperfection of their policy. From the reading, I say, of such books, men have undertaken to kill their kings, because the Greek and Latin writers, in their books and discourses of policy, make it lawful and laudable for any man so to do, provided before he do it, he call him tyrant. For they say not regicide, that is, killing of a king, but tyrannicide, that is, killing of a tyrant, is lawful. From the same books, they that live under a monarch conceive an opinion, that the subjects in a popular Commonwealth enjoy liberty; but that in a monarchy they are all slaves ... In sum, I cannot imagine how anything can be more prejudicial to a monarchy than the allowing of such books to be publicly read, without present applying such correctives of discreet masters as are fit to take away their venom: which venom I will not doubt to compare to the biting of a mad dog, which is a disease that physicians call hydrophobia, or fear of water. For as he that is so bitten has a continual torment of thirst, and yet abhors water; and is in such an estate as if the poison endeavoured to convert him into a dog; so when a monarchy is once bitten to the quick by those democratical writers that continually snarl at that estate; it wants nothing more than a strong monarch, which nevertheless out of a certain tyrannophobia, or

> fear of being strongly governed, when they have him,
> they abhor.
>
> > (*Leviathan*, chapter 29)

Himself foaming a bit, Hobbes nonetheless makes a good point about liberty, and in this particular ideological struggle between freedom as non-interference (Hobbes's view) and freedom as non-dependence (the republican view), it is Hobbes's view that seems to have prevailed in philosophy today. Certainly, the absence of interference seems to be a necessary condition. But is it sufficient? The voices of Hobbes's republican opponents are barely audible now, but as Skinner's archaeology has revealed, they identified something else fundamental about the experience of freedom. If one enjoys one's freedom merely at the grace of a superior, one does not feel free. As James Harrington, one of the most powerful voices from this lost tradition, explained in the Preliminaries to his 1656 book *The Commonwealth of Oceana*: a subject of Constantinople is *not* as free as a citizen of the Italian city-state of Lucca. Taking the juggernaut of *Leviathan* head on, he insists that even the highest noble in Constantinople is still a slave, living at the discretion of the Sultan:
... whereas the greatest bashaw is a tenant, as well as of his head as of his estate, at the will of his lord, the meanest Lucchese that has land is a freeholder of both, and not to be controlled but by the law; and that framed

by every private man unto no other end (or they may thank themselves) than to protect the liberty of every private man, which by that means comes to be the liberty of the commonwealth.'

Thinking beyond the turrets of Lucca to the office blocks of today, don't we all know how oppressive it can be to depend on the goodwill of our boss? How it can make us anxious and uncertain, flattering and flirtatious, our slavery turning us slavish and even constraining our actions when there is no explicit coercion (working late, taking on a task that will run us into the ground, betraying our principles . . .).

I want to end this chapter, as much a lesson from his enemies as it is from Hobbes himself, by wondering whether they themselves missed something ineradicable and sometimes reforming about human relationships. While there is palpably a field of associations of dependence and domination which are enslaving and where power is abused, there are some, for example, if the boss is a good, reasonable and empathetic boss, which can make one a better worker and person. And then there are relationships between equals, when we fruitfully impose our wills upon each other, as when a friend prevails on us to do something we don't want to do for their sake, or when they see better than we do what we ought to do and force us to see it too. Our wills are not always transparent to ourselves, and they can be changed for good as well as bad, and might accordingly be sometimes helpfully cleansed and moulded through interaction with our respectful peers.

# 5

# ON CREATURES
# OF PASSION

..........

Challenging our own as well as his contemporaries' preconceptions about why we do what we do, Hobbes insists that *everything* we do is the effect of our passions. Prising off the grip Aristotelian-Christian doctrine had on the seventeenth century, Hobbes declared that humans are not possessed of a specific rational soul and made in the image of God, but are in many ways just like other animals, motivated by a string of appetites and aversions that lead them through the world in what Hobbes calls voluntary motion. Just as a mouse moves towards the cheese and away from the cat, so we as people edge towards our mate and away from the cliff. When we come across the prospect of something we feel conflicted about, such as an affair, a cigarette or a piece of chocolate cake, we alternate between desire and reluctance before finally deciding. This process of vacillation between passions is what Hobbes calls deliberation, and the last appetite in deliberation is called the will.

When in the mind of man appetites and aversions, hopes and fears, concerning one and the same thing, arise alternately; and diverse good and evil consequences of the doing or omitting the thing propounded come successively into our thoughts; so that sometimes we have an appetite to it, sometimes an aversion from it; sometimes hope to be able to do it, sometimes despair, or fear to attempt it; the whole sum of desires, aversions, hopes and fears, continued till the thing be either done, or thought impossible, is that we call deliberation.

... And it is called deliberation; because it is a putting an end to the liberty we had of doing, or omitting, according to our own appetite, or aversion.

This alternate succession of appetites, aversions, hopes and fears is no less in other living creatures than in man: and therefore beasts also deliberate.

Every deliberation is then said to end, when that whereof they deliberate is either done, or thought impossible; because till then we retain the liberty of doing, or omitting, according to our appetite, or aversion.

In deliberation, the last appetite, or aversion, immediately adhering to the action, or to the omission thereof, is that we call the will; the act (not the faculty) of willing. And beasts that have deliberation, must necessarily also have will. The definition of the will, given commonly by the Schools, that it is a rational appetite, is not good. For if it were, then could there be no voluntary act against reason. For a voluntary act is that which proceeds from the will, and no other. But if instead of a rational appetite, we shall say an appetite resulting from a precedent deliberation, then the definition is the same that I have given here. Will, therefore, is the last appetite in deliberating. And though we say in common discourse, a man had a will once to do a thing, that nevertheless he forbore to do; yet that is properly but an inclination, which makes no action voluntary; because the action depends not of it, but of the last inclination, or appetite. For if the intervenient appetites make any action voluntary, then by the same reason all intervenient aversions should make the same action involuntary; and so one and the same action should be both voluntary and involuntary.

By this it is manifest, that not only actions that have their beginning from covetousness, ambition, lust, or other appetites to the thing propounded; but also those that have their beginning from aversion, or fear of those consequences that follow the omission, are voluntary actions.

(*Leviathan*, chapter 6)

Note how there is no room in this model for what philosophers have termed *akrasia,* or weakness of will, where classically we know what we ought to do, but don't have the will to do it, where our passions trump our reason, and we have the affair or the cigarette. For Hobbes, all actions are equally willed, and all are the result of a chain of passions.

Note too how there is no room here for the freedom of the will. *Deliberation* is precisely that, the removal of the liberty to do something else. Our will is simply the last link in a chain of desires, and all our actions are fully determined by an unbroken series of causes. That Hobbes is a determinist and does not believe in free will, however, does not mean that he does not believe in free human beings, as we know. They are free when their wills (themselves caused) are unimpeded by external impediments.

It is especially important for Hobbes to build this model, not just because he wants to pull down the meta-physical house of the philosophical Establishment, but also because he needs it to legitimate the social contract which lies at the base of his own somewhat tottering political theory. We agree to obey the sovereign, remember, because we are frightened either of our fellow humans in the state of nature, or of that sover-eign himself, already or newly in place. Fear, therefore, is the fulcrum of the State (as well as the passion that is eliminated by it). It is, as Hobbes says punningly, 'the passion to be reckoned upon'. It can be relied upon to make people submit, and it is rational for them to do so (that way they avoid death).

However, one might well object (and people at the time did) that if we enter into a contract out of fear it is not valid – it was coerced, we were not free and therefore we did not really have a choice. If someone puts a knife to my throat and I give him my money, I surely do not do so freely, and may legitimately try to get my money back when I am able. The 'contract' that I seem to have made is therefore void. For Hobbes, however, there is no such thing as coercion. All actions are caused by one passion or another and fear is not a special case, indeed as we've heard Hobbes say, it can be a highly reasonable emotion. He asks us to think of a man on a boat which will sink if he does not throw his bags overboard. Is he constrained when he tosses them out? Oh, no. As Hobbes says, he does so 'very willingly'. Like the man at sea, the man who submits to the sovereign has a choice. He is free to say no, and is therefore obliged by the contract.

Fear and liberty are consistent: as when a man throws his goods into the sea for fear the ship should sink, he doth it nevertheless very willingly, and may refuse to do it if he will; it is therefore the action of one that was free: so a man sometimes pays his debt, only for fear of imprisonment, which, because no body hindered him from detaining, was the action of a man at liberty. And generally all actions which men do in Commonwealths, for fear of the law, are actions which the doers had liberty to omit.

Liberty and necessity are consistent: as in the water that has not only liberty, but a necessity of descending by the channel; so, likewise in the actions which men voluntarily do, which, because they proceed from their will, proceed from liberty; and yet because every act of man's will, and every desire and inclination proceeds from some cause, and that from another cause, in a continual chain (whose first link is in the hand of God, the first of all causes) they proceed from necessity.

(*Leviathan*, chapter 21)

While we'd probably all want to round on Hobbes and insist that there is such a thing as coercion and that coerced actions are by definition unfree, what he does is to show us that these occupy the extreme end of a broad spectrum of actions that do not feel very free but that we are nonetheless responsible for. What he does therefore is to challenge our intuitions about agency. We are all too familiar with the sensation of losing control, of being overwhelmed by our passions. We have all heard the line: 'I was in love; I had no choice.' Hobbes shakes us out of this delusion. There are no excuses. He makes us see that we do not stand, as it were, in front of our actions, able to distance ourselves more or less from them, but that we *are* our actions, even those we'd rather disown.

And pushing in a slightly different direction, he also shows us that our choices are always limited. Goodness knows we'd like to live in a society where every person, not just the lucky few, was given more. But there will always be a limit, and it can be empowering to work with those choices that we have rather than throw up our hands in despair at those that we do not.

This unceasing flow of passions that Hobbes identifies has a further lesson for us. We often want just to STOP. No sooner have we finished one thing, than we want the next – another promotion, another episode of *Mad Men*, another high – and the things that we have been doing do not seem quite to satisfy, to open up on those summer fields where we can loll in deep contentment. We yearn for calm, for a serene nothingness. Hobbes comes crashing in with characteristic realism. Life is desire, you cannot transcend it, so go with it. Stop treading the river water.

Continual success in obtaining those things which a man from time to time desires, that is to say, continual prospering, is that men call felicity; I mean the felicity of this life. For there is no such thing as perpetual tranquillity of mind, while we live here; because life itself is but motion, and can never be without desire, nor without fear, no more than without sense.

(*Leviathan*, chapter 6)

This strikes me as such a captivating point that I'm going to quote another extract which repeats it, this time even more sharply, specifying that one desire which we all share is the ceaseless desire for power – which in turn will enable us to pursue all the other desires which tense our minds.

> ... the felicity of this life consists not in the repose of a mind satisfied. For there is no such *finis ultimus* (utmost aim) nor *summum bonum* (greatest good) as is spoken of in the books of the old moral philosophers. Nor can a man any more live, whose desires are at an end than he whose senses and imaginations are at a stand. Felicity is a continual progress of the desire from one object to another ...
>
> So that in the first place, I put for a general inclination of all mankind a perpetual and restless desire of power after power, that ceases only in death.
>
> (*Leviathan*, chapter 11)

Hobbes's words resonate especially loudly, eerily, for us now in our own speeded-up technological, panoptical and consumerist age. The prospect of tranquillity seems even more remote for us, as desire after desire – to own that dress, to look that good, to be included in a well-Tweeted party, to answer this email now – is beamed into our computers, our phones, our high streets. Indeed, this new fast flow of passion and perception that bears us along feels sometimes as though it might drown us, or certainly drown out other more fulfilling passions.

# 6

# ON GOODNESS
# (FOR ME AND FOR YOU)

..........

These coursing, directing passions provide the life-
blood for both a riotous and a robust ethics. As we will
see, Hobbes begins from an apparently relativist position which then flowers into moral knowledge, striking
many as contradictory but perhaps precisely thereby
capturing something of the sandy soil out of which full-
blown morality can and must grow.

Just as the colour blue is not in the sky, but in the
person who looks at the sky, so 'good' and 'bad' are
not in things themselves but simply perceptions of
those things. We call something 'good', says Hobbes,
because we like it, we desire it, because it is good *for
us*. And because my desires clash with yours, and we
disagree about what is good and what is bad, it seems
that there is no common, let alone real, morality, which
is why sometimes a third party is needed to adjudicate
between competing claims.

And because the constitution of a man's body is in
continual mutation; it is impossible that all the same

things should always cause in him the same appetites and aversions: much less can all men consent
in the desire of almost any one and the same object.

But whatsoever is the object of any man's appetite or desire; that is it, which he for his part calls
good; and the object of his hate and aversion, evil;
and of his contempt, vile and inconsiderable. For
these words of good, evil, and contemptible are
ever used with relation to the person that uses
them: there being nothing simply and absolutely
so; nor any common rule of good and evil, to be
taken from the nature of the objects themselves;
but from the person of the man (where there is no
Commonwealth); or, in a Commonwealth from the
person that represents it; or from an arbitrator or
judge, whom men disagreeing shall by consent set
up and make his sentence the rule thereof.

(*Leviathan*, chapter 6)

So desperate is this state of conflicting passions, this moral chaos wherein everyone thinks they know better than everyone else and each is sure that they have right on their side, that we need to find a way out. Hobbes's solution is that while we seem to disagree about almost everything else, we all agree on one thing: we do not want to die.

We share these basic overwhelming passions: the fear of death and the desire to survive and thrive. No one

– unless they are mad – is without these desires. They are incontrovertible goods for all, and therefore provide a sure footing on which to build a genuinely common morality. We work out that if we want to live (which we all do) then we must seek peace. This is the bedrock axiom of moral science. Having calculated it, our reason can then deduce with irrefutable certainty all the ways in which we can achieve that goal. These dictates of reason turn out to be nothing less than the good old Christian laws of nature (the commands of God, understood by Hobbes as the author or first cause of our nature) as well as the full gamut of the conventional Renaissance virtues, and Thomas Hobbes, branded both sceptic and atheist, can sit back and announce that he has produced a universally and eternally true morality.

> The passions that incline men to peace are: fear of death; desire of such things as are necessary to commodious living; and a hope by their industry to obtain them. And reason suggests convenient articles of peace, upon which men may be drawn to agreement. These articles are they which otherwise are called the laws of nature . . .
>
> (*Leviathan*, chapter 13)

We saw Hobbes begin his deductions in chapter two: if the first law of nature is to seek peace, then the second must be that, since war is caused by everyone having the right to anything, each person must promise to lay down theirs on the condition that the others do the same. It follows that, if this promise is to hold, the third law must be that people honour their promises. This is recognizably the great virtue of 'justice' – the keeping of contracts, of giving each their due. The fourth law is that people who receive a free gift (sovereign, take note) ought not to make the giver regret that gift. This is 'gratitude'. Hobbes goes on to infer a total of nineteen duties, all of which are scientifically verifiable insofar as they are the causes of peace. They include being sociable, forgiving, polite, modest, equitable and impartial; punishing with a view to rehabilitation rather than retribution; acknowledging each other as equal; and being willing to submit to arbitration when controversies cannot be internally resolved. Not only are many of these familiar as the stock list of ancient virtues but, venturing even deeper into the enemy camp and stealing the treasure, Hobbes declares with a smile that they can all be summed up by the Christian golden rule: do unto others as you'd have done unto yourself (although Hobbes turns it into the negative form, playing yet more with the tradition he is seeming to support).

These are the laws of nature, dictating peace, for a means of the conservation of men in multitudes; and which only concern the doctrine of civil society.

There be other things tending to the destruction of particular men; as drunkenness . . .

And though this may seem too subtle a deduction of the laws of nature to be taken notice of by all men, whereof the most part are too busy in getting food, and the rest too negligent to understand; yet to leave all men inexcusable, they have been contracted into one easy sum, intelligible even to the meanest capacity; and that is: Do not that to another which thou would not have done to thyself; which shows him that he has no more to do in learning the laws of nature but, when weighing the actions of other men with his own, they seem too heavy, to put them into the other part of the balance, and his own into their place, that his own passions and self-love may add nothing to the weight; and then there is none of these laws of nature that will not appear unto him very reasonable . . .

The laws of nature are immutable and eternal; for injustice, ingratitude, arrogance, pride, iniquity, acception of persons, and the rest can never be made lawful. For it can never be that war shall preserve life, and peace destroy it.

The same laws, because they oblige only to a desire, and endeavour, mean an unfeigned and constant endeavour, are easy to be observed. For in that they require nothing but endeavour, he that endeavours their performance fulfils them; and he that fulfils the law is just.

And the science of them is the true and only moral philosophy. For moral philosophy is nothing else but the science of what is good and evil in the conversation and society of mankind. Good and evil are names that signify our appetites and aversions; which in different tempers, customs, and doctrines of men are different: and diverse men differ not only in their judgement on the senses of what is pleasant and unpleasant to the taste, smell, hearing, touch, and sight; but also of what is conformable or disagreeable to reason in the actions of common life. Nay, the same man, in diverse times, differs from himself; and one time praises, that is, calls good, what another time he dispraises, and calls evil: from whence arise disputes, controversies, and at last war. And therefore so long [as] a man is in the condition of mere nature, which is a condition of war, private appetite is the measure of good and evil: and consequently all men agree on this, that peace is good, and therefore also the way or means of peace, which (as I have shown before) are justice, gratitude, modesty, equity, mercy, and the rest of the laws of nature, are good; that is to say, moral virtues; and their contrary vices, evil. Now the science of virtue and vice is moral philosophy; and therefore the true doctrine of the laws of nature is the true moral philosophy . . .

These dictates of reason men used to call by the name of laws, but improperly: for they are but conclusions, or theorems concerning what conduces to the conservation and defence of themselves; whereas law, properly, is the word of him that by right has command over others. But yet if we consider the same theorems, as delivered in the word of God, that by right commands all things, then are they properly called laws.

(*Leviathan*, chapter 15)

In another audacious act of literary acrobatics therefore, Hobbes grounds the moral pieties of his contemporaries in rational demonstration and subjective passions. Many commentators have found this cynical, asking what kind of moral obligations these are that can be broken when they come at a cost to ourselves, that begin and end with egoism. Certainly there are many other ways to think about goodness. But Hobbes seems to me to put down some important markers.

From the way we talk, often quite reasonably – 'dropping litter is bad', 'honesty is good', 'he is evil' – anyone would think that there really are moral facts out there. Hobbes reminds us that we make them up. This is not to say that they don't matter, and that we cannot make them up better (or worse), but rather that they are contingent projections that we humans cast over the world. There is a distinction between facts and values that our language often obscures. Badness for example is not *in* the act of dropping litter in the way that the falling sweet wrapper is in the act.

Hobbes shows us the deep connection between our desires and our duties – not so much in the crude sense that he has seemed to many readers to have gestured towards the theory of enlightened self-interest, whereby I work out that if I am nice to you, you'll be nice to me, although of course reciprocity plays its part in practical reasoning. Rather, I mean that Hobbes points us to the way in which our ethical frameworks draw heavily on our emotional judgements about what is important, which often converge, so that the good for me is also the good for you.

Pulling us away from moral fantasies, he also draws our attention to the fragility of moral culture, to the way that it needs the supportive artifice of the State to stand tall, or else be turned completely on its head:

> To this war of every man against every man, this also is consequent; that nothing can be unjust. The notions of right and wrong, justice and injustice, have there no place. Where there is no common power, there is no law; where no law, no injustice. Force and fraud are in war the two cardinal virtues. Justice and injustice are none of the faculties neither of the body, nor mind. If they were, they might be in a man that were alone in the world, as well as his senses and passions. They are qualities that relate to men in society, not in solitude. It is consequent also to the same condition that there be no propriety, no

dominion, no mine and thine distinct; but only that to be every man's that he can get, and for so long as he can keep it. And thus much for the ill condition which man by mere nature is actually placed in; though with a possibility to come out of it, consisting partly in the passions, partly in his reason.

(*Leviathan*, chapter 13)

Even in a well-functioning State – or office, or household – our rallying partiality, our trenchant conviction that we are in the right, often requires a third party to smooth out the collisions between normative descriptions that will inevitably arise:

And as in arithmetic unpractised men must, and professors themselves may often, err, and cast up false; so also in any other subject of reasoning, the ablest, most attentive, and most practised men may deceive themselves, and infer false conclusions; not but that reason itself is always right reason, as well as arithmetic is a certain and infallible art: but no one man's reason, nor the reason of any one number of men, makes the certainty; no more than an account is therefore well cast up, because a great many men have unanimously approved it. And therefore, as when there is a controversy in an account, the parties must by their own accord set up for right reason the reason of some arbitrator, or judge, to whose sentence they will both stand, or their controversy must either come to blows, or be undecided, for want of a right reason constituted by Nature; so is it also in all debates of what kind soever: and when men that think themselves wiser than all others clamour and demand right reason for judge; yet seek no more but that things should be determined by no other men's reason but their own, it is as intolerable in the society of men, as it is in play after trump is turned to use for trump on every occasion, that suit whereof they have most in their hand. For they do nothing else, that will have every of their passions, as it comes to bear sway in them, to be taken for right reason, and that in their own controversies: bewrays their want of right reason by the claim they lay to it.

(*Leviathan*, chapter 5)

What Hobbes helps us to see are the dangers of taking too quickly to the moral high ground. My goodness we all know how nice it can be up there, sitting around at a dinner party for example, enjoying the breeze of self-congratulation, joining in the chorus of disapproval for the way that someone parents, or for what they buy, or how they vote, or who they sleep with. Hobbes prompts us to remember that neither you nor I have a monopoly on right, that instead our individual viewpoints are highly subjective, that what we believe is heavily influenced by our passions and interests, by what it is convenient, convivial, and easy to believe. Each person often thinks that they have good reasons for doing what they do, and are sure that they are in the right. And it's not just that we should as a result at least try to be a little more tolerant and respectful of difference (without descending into an equally anti-social nihilism), but that we should own up to our own corruption, even if that is only (and of course it never is) our rather viperous tendency to judge others. And finally, remember Hobbes's injunction to follow peace. Sociability is in itself a good, and there's virtue in rubbing along politely even with those whose opinions we despise.

# 7

# ON THE DANGERS
# OF WORDS

..........

One lesson that has cropped up already and on which I shall now focus is Hobbes's warning about the duplicitous and hazardous power of language. Words give the illusion of objectivity, of right reason, whereas in fact they are often saturated with subjectivity and error, with the way things appear to us or the way that we want them to be, rather than the way they actually are. We say, for example, that the sky is blue, the will free, and this or that good or evil, when the first is absurd, the second mistaken, and the third simply an expression of our desires. The great problem with words, however, is that they have the appearance, the assertion, of veracity. If we are not careful, they make the world in their own image. They float free of their objects and can be applied as we choose and as it serves our interests, so that for instance we might call a person 'cruel' when they are in fact 'just', and thereby legitimize action against them. It is the figure of the rhetorician whom Hobbes has in his sights at this juncture, especially those orators who whip up such a frenzy in Parliament and the pulpit, and who by their

> art of words ... represent to others, that which is
> Good, in the likeness of Evil; and Evil, in the likeness
> of Good; and augment, or diminish the apparent
> greatnesse of Good and Evil; discontenting men, and
> troubling their peace at their pleasure.
>
> (*Leviathan*, chapter 17)

Words themselves therefore can elicit strong emotions to devastating effect. We have already seen how labelling someone a 'tyrant' can cost him his head. To take another of Hobbes's examples, 'that reverenced name of conscience' can, when affixed to a flimsy opinion, or perhaps to the justification for informing on a rival, put these prosaic iterations beyond reproach. And as if being indeterminate and emotive were not enough, words can conjure something out of nothing, creating entities that are no more than fantasies, and exist simply because powerful people say they do. Hobbes lays into the dominant metaphysics of the time, which raves on about the 'abstract essences' of things, those 'substantial forms' separated from bodies which he thinks are such a nonsense, and which not only pollute the avid masses with insignificant noise, but which terrify them into thinking that they see ghosts in graveyards, or dupe them into believing that the bread they chew in church is Jesus Christ himself. The 'empty names' are no more than scarecrows, but just as effective.

What is particularly incisive about Hobbes's analysis of language is that he identifies the bewitching power of words not simply on other people, but on ourselves as well. They cast their spell on all of us, seeming to deliver the truth. We need to snuff out their false lights, and cleanse them of equivocation, so that they act as a window on to the world, rather than a mirror which reflects back only our vain impressions.

Seeing then that truth consists in the right ordering of names in our affirmations, a man that seeks precise truth had need to remember what every name he uses stands for, and to place it accordingly; or else he will find himself entangled in words, as a bird in lime twigs; the more he struggles, the more belimed. And therefore in geometry (which is the only science that it has pleased God hitherto to bestow on mankind), men begin at settling the significations of their words; which settling of significations, they call definitions, and place them in the beginning of their reckoning.

By this it appears how necessary it is for any man that aspires to true knowledge, to examine the definitions of former authors; and either to correct them, where they are negligently set down, or to make them himself. For the errors of definitions multiply themselves, according as the reckoning proceeds, and lead men into absurdities, which at last they see, but cannot avoid, without reckoning anew from the beginning; in which lies the foundation of their errors. From whence it happens that they which trust to books do as they that cast up many little sums into a greater, without considering whether those little sums were rightly cast up or not; and at last finding the error visible, and not mistrusting their first grounds, know not which way to clear themselves, but spend time in fluttering over their books; as birds that entering by the chimney, and finding themselves enclosed in a chamber, flutter at the false light of a glass window, for want of wit to consider which way they came in. So that in the right definition of names lies the first use of speech; which is the acquisition of science: and in wrong, or no definitions, lies the first abuse; from which proceed all false and senseless tenets; which make those men that take their instruction from the authority of books, and not from their own meditation, to be as much below the condition of ignorant men as men endued with true science are above it. For between true science and erroneous doctrines, ignorance is in the middle. Natural sense and imagination are not subject to absurdity. Nature itself cannot err: and as men abound in copiousness of language; so they become more wise, or more mad, than ordinary. Nor is it possible without letters for any man to become either excellently wise or (unless his memory be hurt by disease, or ill constitution of organs) excellently foolish. For words are wise men's counters; they do but reckon by them: but they are the money of fools, that value them by the authority of an Aristotle, a Cicero, or a Thomas, or any other doctor whatsoever, if but a man.

(*Leviathan*, chapter 4)

Words, then, can be like fool's gold – glinting seductively but meaning nothing at all.

Interweaving now the previous lesson with this one, words are also infused with our highly partial moral perspectives. Applying loaded words at will and as it serves our turn, we draft highly arbitrary maps of values.

The names of such things as affect us, that is, which please and displease us, because all men be not alike affected with the same thing, nor the same man at all times, are in the common discourses of men of inconstant signification. For seeing all names are imposed to signify our conceptions; and all our affections are but conceptions; when we conceive the same things differently, we can hardly avoid different naming of them. For though the nature of that we conceive be the same; yet the diversity of our reception of it, in respect of different constitutions of body and prejudices of opinion, gives everything a tincture of our different passions. And therefore in reasoning, a man must take heed of words; which, besides the signification of what we imagine of their nature, have a signification also of the nature, disposition, and interest of the speaker; such as are the names of virtues and vices: for one man calls wisdom, what another calls fear; and one cruelty, what another justice; one prodigality, what another magnanimity; and one gravity, what another stupidity, etc. And therefore such names can never be true grounds of any ratiocination. No more can metaphors and tropes of speech: but these are less dangerous because they profess their inconstancy, which the other do not.

(*Leviathan*, chapter 4)

In one of my favourite extracts, Hobbes, himself no stranger to the killer metaphor, goes on to exhort us to wash our words clean, dyed as they are with passion, interest and error.

To conclude, the light of humane minds is perspicuous words, but by exact definitions first snuffed, and purged from ambiguity; reason is the pace; increase of science, the way; and the benefit of mankind, the end. And, on the contrary, metaphors, and senseless and ambiguous words are like *ignes fatui* [will-o'-the-wisps]; and reasoning upon them is wandering

amongst innumerable absurdities; and their end,
contention and sedition, or contempt.

(*Leviathan*, chapter 5)

The constitutive power of words, the way they shape truth, is something about which we should be vigilant. The problem is perhaps not so pressing in the case of the natural world, which pushes back against obviously outlandish descriptions. However, while it is hard to get away with calling the earth flat (although some people do), it is easy to re-describe the moral world, often with desperate consequences, as for example when a person is described as a 'terrorist', rather than a 'freedom fighter'. Governments the world over are employed in these kinds of potent linguistic manipulations. By naming something 'good', they make it so, and thereby legitimize or excuse all manner of destruction. The US, for example, began by calling its 'War on Terror' a 'Crusade' and 'Operation Infinite Justice', and then (when they realized they hadn't got the language quite right) the official code name they gave the 'intervention' in Afghanistan in October 2001 was 'Operation Enduring Freedom', even as the bombs dropped. The lexicon subsequently turned even more obscure as 'collateral damage' and 'extraordinary rendition' entered the fray. Closer to home, single mothers are labelled 'irresponsible' rather than, for example, 'brave and resourceful', and benefit claimants 'scroungers' rather than 'vulnerable and in legitimate need'. This kind of creative naming is all the more effective in our Tweeting, electronic age, as words can be all the more quickly, unthinkingly and unaccountably attached to things.

And if we turn from the public sphere (where perhaps we'd expect battles of ideology to match battles of power), to the warm hearth of the family, we find that there too we're engaged in acts of linguistic creation. Indeed, parents, themselves jointly the sovereign in a family, name things – 'nasty' and 'nice', as well as 'tree' and 'cup' – and shape the world that their children inhabit. If we are not attentive, we spend too much time calling our daughters 'beautiful', and our sons 'clever', and thereby define for them what they essentially are and ought to be.

Hobbes's lesson is that it is not only other people's words that we should be suspicious of, but our own. 'Nosce teipsum, Read thy self', he instructs us in the introduction to Leviathan. Bore into the words that make us who we are, and ensure that they make sense.

# 8

# ON RELIGION AS A
# HUMAN CONSTRUCT

..........

It is difficult to work out what Hobbes thought about
Christianity, and reading him on the subject is a bit like
trying to decipher a palimpsest: not only does what he
says point us in different directions, but we cannot be
sure what he thinks. On the one hand, he wanted to
win over a generally devout audience and might therefore be less devout than he at times appears. On the
other, he lived in an age drenched in faith, when it
would have been unthinkable to be an atheist in our
sense of the term, and so his sceptical notes ring more
radically than perhaps they should in our own sceptical
ears. Rather than head off down this murky track (and
heaven knows, the last thing you need, dear reader,
is a lesson about whether God exists), I've extracted
Hobbes's remarkable and relatively self-contained
anthropological analysis of the origins of religion.

It has its seeds, he says, in human nature, and
sprouts because we do not understand how the world
works, why for example an earthquake or a storm or
gravity occurs, and so we infer, or invent, some cause

(we might call it God, or Allah, or pixie) that we imagine brings them about. This curiosity into the causes of inexplicable phenomena is one of the few things that marks human beings out from other animals, and the reason why we alone in nature seem to have the idea of a god. Unlike other beasts, who are caught up in the moment, in the food, rest and sex they are having today, we are highly exercised by the past and the future, and ultimately the death to come, sometimes to our benefit but frequently, in the context of religion, to our cost.

This distinctively human inquisition into the chain of cause and effect can take the soaring form of science, and end up with the inference that, in this mechanical universe, there must be a first and eternal cause without which the earth would not turn, and which one might quite properly call 'God'. More often, however, our predispositions to both hindsight and foresight turn us inside out with fear of the invisible causes which rock our lives, and of what they might do to us tomorrow or when we die. Will I get pregnant before I'm too old? Will I get cancer? Will I go to hell? What is this mighty unseen power that plays so fast and loose with my fate? Hobbes compares these gut-wrenching anxieties to the suffering of Prometheus. Every day his liver was picked at by an eagle, and every night it regenerated, just as our unease pauses only, if we're lucky, in sleep. In this angst-ridden state, we have neither time nor inclination for science, but slip instead into superstition, fabricating all sorts of beings and charms which we imagine to be the agents of our fortune. Unable to admit that we have no understanding of these potent causes we call spirits or sprites, we see them everywhere, in cemeteries and rabbits' feet, and become in turn more afraid. We fall prey to preachers and priests who claim to understand them and how to placate them, and so play on our fretful credulity to gain power over us and the State. They are conjurors and liars, however, says Hobbes, and it is his mission to shatter their enchantment. He trains his dry wit for example on the case of the visionary:

> To say [God] has spoken to him in a dream, is no more than to say he has dreamt that God spake to him.
>
> (*Leviathan*, chapter 32)

With his critique of religion, then, Hobbes has brought us full circle. We began these lessons with the problem of fear and Hobbes's desire to expunge it. By bringing his pen to bear on organized and enthusiastic 'worship', he has completed his task.

> Ignorance of natural causes disposes a man to credulity, so as to believe many times impossibilities: for such know nothing to the contrary, but that they may be true, being unable to detect the

impossibility. And credulity, because men love to be hearkened unto in company, disposes them to lying: so that ignorance itself, without malice, is able to make a man both to believe lies and tell them, and sometimes also to invent them.

Anxiety for the future time disposes men to inquire into the causes of things: because the knowledge of them makes men the better able to order the present to their best advantage.

Curiosity, or love of the knowledge of causes, draws a man from consideration of the effect to seek the cause; and again, the cause of that cause; till of necessity he must come to this thought at last, that there is some cause whereof there is no former cause, but is eternal; which is it men call God. So that it is impossible to make any profound inquiry into natural causes without being inclined thereby to believe there is one God eternal; though they cannot have any idea of Him in their mind answerable to His nature. For as a man that is born blind, hearing men talk of warming themselves by the fire, and being brought to warm himself by the same, may easily conceive, and assure himself, there is somewhat there which men call fire and is the cause of the heat he feels, but cannot imagine what it is like, nor have an idea of it in his mind such as they have that see it: so also, by the visible things of this world, and their admirable order, a man may conceive there is a cause of them, which men call God, and yet not have an idea or image of Him in his mind.

And they that make little or no inquiry into the natural causes of things, yet from the fear that proceeds from the ignorance itself of what it is that has the power to do them much good or harm, are inclined to suppose, and feign unto themselves, several kinds of powers invisible; and to stand in awe of their own imaginations, and in time of distress to invoke them; as also in the time of unexpected good success, to give them thanks; making the creatures of their own fancy, their gods. By which means it has come to pass that from the innumerable variety of fancy, men have created in the world innumerable sorts of gods. And this fear of things invisible is the natural seed of that which every one in himself calls religion; and in them that worship or fear that power otherwise than they do, superstition.

And this seed of religion, having been observed by many, some of those that have observed it have been inclined thereby to nourish, dress, and form it into laws; and to add to it, of their own invention, any opinion of the causes of future events by which they thought they should best be able to govern others, and make unto themselves the greatest use of their powers.

(*Leviathan*, chapter 11)

It is, as so often with Hobbes, hard not to be struck by the seeming modernity of his words. They speak to us perhaps particularly urgently, precisely because we find our modern selves in an oddly reinvigorated religious age and therefore with a kind of telescope which can make out more clearly now Hobbes's own witch-hunting, Bible-bashing age. In Mississippi as in Karachi, in London as in Tehran, preachers are drawing ever larger crowds, and fundamentalism is on the rise. And as Hobbes had observed, where there's organized religion, there's also domination and oppression – of gay people who are excluded from the sacrament of marriage, of women who are not permitted (high) office or contraception, of adulterers who are stoned to death.

# CONCLUSION:
# WHAT PRICE PEACE?

..........

'Are you mad?' we might reply to Hobbes. Instead of freeing us from fear, he is surely ratcheting it up by creating a monster far more terrifying than anything one or two men in the state of nature could muster. As John Locke, one of Hobbes's most influential critics, observed in his *Two Treatises of Government* (published in 1689), to give the sovereign absolute power because one fears one's fellow subjects, is to worry more about polecats and foxes, only to find oneself in the lion's den.

Certainly, the yoke of government can weigh too punishingly on people and there are times when we must try to shake it off, and even some times when outsiders have an obligation to intervene. Sometimes the costs of 'order' overbalance the benefits. As I heard an Afghan woman say on the radio about the prospect of American talks with the Taliban: she wants peace, yes, but not at any price, thank you all the same. And of course 'peace' itself is a contested term and never means peace for everyone, especially not for minority or marginalized groups. Indeed, famously, it can be used as a nice word to cover a mass slaughter, as in the Roman conquest of Britain. 'Where they make a desert, they call it peace', is Tacitus's sentence as it is often translated, referring to precisely the kind of pernicious and powerful word-play which Hobbes himself despises.

I am not going to defend Hobbes here. His stark prohibition on anything but the narrowest individual right of resistance, together with his endorsement of the unlimited rights of government, are as obscene as they are indefensible. It has been especially hard to write this book in the extraordinary flowering of the Arab spring, when all our hearts have gone out to the courageous women and men who have taken to the streets and parks of Tunisia, Egypt, Libya, Yemen, Syria and Bahrain, and stood up for their undoubted rights in wave upon deadly wave.

Along the road to hell, however, Hobbes does seem to me to have got a handle on the nature of the State, and the peculiar significance of war and peace, and I shall end by rounding up his lessons on these.

Like it or not, what the modern State has, and apparently has to have if it is to function, is a monopoly of force, however controlled by the rule of law. Only if Leviathan roars can he truly be 'King of the Proud'. This idea, as unsettling as it is compelling, is one that Hobbes formulated with peculiar precision, and liberalism has never been able to shake it off.

More humanely now, Hobbes is also a witness to the peculiar horror of civil war, and just as we should listen to those civilians in conflicts in our own day who say they want peace above all things, so we should hear his testimony. Locke had the fortune to be writing when the memory of the all-out bloodbath of the 1640s was fading. Hobbes did not have this luck. Where we happen to find ourselves standing in history makes a huge difference to what we think is important, and sometimes our view is blocked of what is equally or more important.

Let us turn now from full-scale war to arguments at home, at work or in the pub; not only the fierce fights which feel like they might tear us apart, but the trivial ones too which somehow manage to incense us all the same – that chair is mine, not yours; *Girls* IS a really good television show; no, Hobbes *does* think that there's a distinction between the sovereign and the State; God exists, no he doesn't. We burn with the knowledge that we are in the right, or that we are right, and that therefore the right thing to do is to keep on fighting, the flames of certainty fanned by pride and self-interest. It can feel as though there's no way out, that we've fallen down a hole that threatens to swallow us up. The liberating lesson from Hobbes is that often the right thing to do is to make peace, that the object of the argument is often less important than the relationship at stake. Once we see this, and agree, or apologize, we can escape the battle, and quickly feel the relief flooding in, indeed (although this can be another rabbit hole) we can even feel a bit good about ourselves. Points of information, as well as points of principle, are often highly subjective, even in the brave new world of Google and the iPhone, and they generally pale in comparison not only to the joy of generous interaction, but also to the freedom from the interminable and blinding logic of an argument, from the acid mood which sours us.

One way of seeing the precise significance of peace, that thing without which our lives would be impoverished but which we tend to take for granted – is to compare it to sleep. This too is fundamental to our happiness, but because it is generally available we do not appreciate it enough. If we are lucky, and fall, evening after evening, quickly into sleep and stay in it till morning, we do not even think about it. If, on the other hand, we have had the thought, in the heart-pounding, eyes-wide-open horror of the middle of the night, that the sensible thing to do would be to run into the wall and knock ourselves out, and so bring the sweet relief of unconsciousness, we know the gift that sleep is. Peace is a gift, too, and we should not give it up lightly. Indeed, sleep is not just an analogy for peace, but it is another thing that depends on it. Peace really is among the deepest goods. How much are we prepared to pay for it?

# HOMEWORK

## 1

### ON LIVING IN FEAR
..........

The extracts from Hobbes's *Leviathan* have been modernized to make them more accessible. They are based on Richard Tuck's 1996 excellent edition of the original 1651 text. The definitive edition is now Noel Malcolm's astonishing 2012 three-volume work for the Clarendon Edition of the Works of Thomas Hobbes.

As it says on the tin, my book looks to the present, but most of the best work on Hobbes has its eye trained on the past, in the eternally relevant discipline of history. The field of Hobbes scholarship is vast, and the following intellectual biographies and collections of essays by many of the world's leading commentators provide brilliant and contradictory insights, as well as introductions to his own enormous *oeuvre*: *Hobbes: A very short introduction* (2002) by Richard Tuck; *Hobbes* (1991) by Tom Sorell; *The Cambridge Companion to Hobbes* (1996), edited by Tom Sorell; *The Cambridge Companion to Hobbes's* Leviathan, edited by Patricia Spingborg (2007); *The Bloomsbury Companion to Hobbes* (2012) and *Hobbes Today: Insights for the 21st Century* (2012), both edited by S. A. Lloyd.

The dismembering horror of war and a Stateless society, which lie at the base of Hobbes's political theory and which he entreats us to keep in view when we feel the violations of government and the itch of revolution, are mercilessly paraded before us in Picasso's painting *Guernica* (1937), Goya's *Disasters of War* drawings (1810–23), and Cormac McCarthy's novel *The Road* (2006). The incomparable television epic *Deadwood* (2004–6) is about what happens when you bring the State to the state of nature of the American Frontier, and it could have been made to illuminate Hobbes's ideas on the perils of lawlessness and the yearning for order. It suggests, however, that while anarchy is an awful place to live, justice, when it comes, suffers multiple and inevitable corruptions and power will always win out, however it is attired. The almost as brilliant *Sopranos* (1999–2007) is also peppered with Hobbesian echoes, most explicitly perhaps in 'Bust Out' (S2E10), when an unfortunate witness to a mafia crime, who is pictured reading Robert Nozick's *Anarchy, State and Utopia* (1974) in his spare time, is made to rue the minimal State. Steven Pinker's *The Better Angels of Our Nature* (2011) suggests, like Hobbes, that with the coming of civilization we become not only safer, but better human beings. And for a classic and hilarious rebuttal of Hobbes and all his heirs, read the wonderful Jean Jacques Rousseau on how it is in fact civilization that has corrupted us (*Of the Social Contract* (1762) and

*Discourse on The Origin and the Foundations of Inequality Among Men* (1755)).

# 2

## ON LIVING WITHOUT FEAR

..........

While the eloquence of democracy and liberalism has charged with exhilarating results against Hobbes, various writers have pointed out that while authoritarianism is not any kind of answer to the problem of societal disorder, politics is, and politics is inevitably at times a matter more of force than of right. One extreme, explicitly Hobbesian, voice is that of Carl Schmitt, who argued in his essay on the subject that 'dictatorship' is a necessary part of politics. In a very different register, Joseph Schumpeter's *Capitalism, Socialism and Democracy* (1942) exposed the myth of 'rule by the people' in a 'democracy'. For a penetrating history of democracy which charts its failures and disingenuities as starkly as it does its on-going appeal, read John Dunn's *Setting the People Free: The Story of Democracy* (2005). And for the (non-existent?) democratic lineaments in Hobbes, read Kinch Hoekstra's and Richard Tuck's fascinating contributions to the overarchingly excellent *Rethinking the Foundations of Modern Political Thought* (2006), edited by Annabel Brett and James Tully.

There are many great works of literature which break Hobbes's spell. Two are: Hans Fallada's *Alone in Berlin* (2009) about lone resistance to Nazi tyranny in 1940s Berlin, and Yevgeny Zamyatin's *We* (1924) about faceless life under a totalitarian regime.

## 3
## ON BEING FREE
..........

To know that Hobbesian freedom is not enough, one only needs to listen to the testimonies of Aung San Suu Kyi, for example in her 2011 BBC Radio 4 Reith Lectures on liberty and dissent, or Desmond Tutu on *Desert Island Discs* on the same channel (itself a bastion of democracy), or Edward Snowden at http://www.youtube.com/watch?v=5yB3n9fu-rM. Coming at the same point from a different angle is Amartya Sen's *Freedom as Development* (1999).

To know that Hobbesian freedom is *something*, one might look at Chagall's picture *The Promenade* (1917–18) which, even mirroring *Leviathan's* own frontispiece with its giant figure ascendant over the countryside, evokes the simple pleasure of enjoying air and motion. It is generally the revolutionaries, the underdogs, who have all the best lines, but 'Me and Bobby McGee' makes the striking point that freedom is an overrated concept, a synonym for nothing left to lose. The song itself has nothing to do with Hobbes, but it's a good song, especially when sung by Janis Joplin, and it evokes Hobbes's insight that constraint can be a good thing. Indeed, there is a computer program called 'Freedom', which knows that some of us need to be restrained from going online, and thereby forces us (frees us) to focus on more rewarding things.

On the question of the value of modern human rights discourse, read Ronald Dworkin's *Taking Rights Seriously* (1977), and then Onora O'Neill's 'The dark side of human rights' (2005) at www.chathamhouse.org.

# 4
## ON FEELING FREE
..........

I owe this chapter to the work of Quentin Skinner, whose books *Hobbes and Republican Liberty* (2008) and *Liberty before Liberalism* (1998) reveal with crystal clarity how Hobbes's changing views on liberty emerge in part out of his refutation of the 'republican' view. For a classic defence of this view, see John Locke's *Second Treatise of Government* (1689), where he declares that the 'freedom of men under government' is 'not to be subject to the inconstant, uncertain, unknown, arbitrary will of another man'. For a modern revival of this tradition, see Philip Pettit's *Republicanism: a theory of freedom and government* (1997).

I cannot leave this chapter without mentioning Nina Simone's 'I wish I knew how it would feel to be free'. It comes to me often, and though again not strictly relevant, it makes it viscerally obvious that Hobbes has not captured all that it means to feel free.

## 5
## ON CREATURES OF PASSION
..........

*Passion and Action* (1997) by Susan James is a stunning analysis of the emotions in Hobbes's time. In the present, Peggy Orenstein's book *Waiting for Daisy* (2007) and the film *Touching the Void* (2003) both provide first-hand proof of Hobbes's claim that, while our lives are continuously – in these two cases extremely – hemmed in by deterministic chains of cause and effect and driven on by the unceasing pressure of our passions, we almost always have choices and these can be liberating. The first case is the story of a woman who is fighting to have a baby against the odds of infertility, and the second of a man who finds himself dangling from a climbing rope in the Andes.

## 6
## ON GOODNESS (FOR ME AND FOR YOU)
..........

Massively indebted to Hobbes, and himself another colossus in Anglophone philosophy, David Hume elaborated a naturalistic ethic which it is even now hard to ignore. You will find this, as well as much more, in his *Treatise of Human Nature* (1739–40) and *Enquiry*

*Concerning the Principles of Morals* (1751). Indebted in his turn to Hume, Simon Blackburn's *Ruling Passions* (2000) sees off scepticism and relativism while developing his own account of the deep connection between passions and morality. For a refreshingly accessible tour through the history of ethics, pick up his *Being Good: A Short Introduction to Ethics* (2002).

# 7

## ON THE DANGERS OF WORDS
..........

In *Reason and Rhetoric in the Philosophy of Thomas Hobbes* (1996), Quentin Skinner demonstrates the importance of Hobbes's attack on eloquence. The false lights of language dazzle and dominate us still. With characteristic clear-sightedness, David Runciman in *Political Hypocrisy: The Mask of Power from Hobbes to Orwell and Beyond* (2008), argues that hypocrisy is a fact of politics, and rather than delude ourselves that we can eradicate it, we should learn how to distinguish between harmless and genuinely pernicious inauthenticity. George Orwell's *Animal Farm* (1945) remains a devastating account of how the ruling class misrepresents reality and protects their privilege with the weapons of words. For more recent, chilling accounts of linguistic *Fiat*, see Joanna Kavenna's *The Birth of Love* (2010) on how the language and therefore the experience of maternity is controlled and manipulated, and Iain Sinclair's *Ghost Milk: Calling*

*Time on the Grand Project* (2011) on how the promise of 'regeneration' can conceal exactly the opposite.

## 8
## ON RELIGION AS A HUMAN CONSTRUCT
..........

Like Hobbes, Daniel Dennett, in *Breaking the Spell: Religion as a Natural Phenomenon* (2006), finds the seeds of religion in human nature. And finally, in a different register entirely, there's Dory Previn's song 'Mythical Kings and Iguanas', which asserts what is lost in the search for spirituality.

# ACKNOWLEDGEMENTS

..........

My greatest debt is to my teachers, Annabel Brett and Quentin Skinner, who taught me as a student how to read Hobbes historically and on his own terms. In writing this book I have had to turn myself inside out slightly and I pray that I have not overly translated Hobbes in the result.

I am hugely grateful to Juliette Mitchell and all those at The School of Life who set me on this unexpected course in the first place and then provided me with such encouragement; to Mark Bearn and Vladimir Eatwell, who each read drafts of the book and gave me invaluable comments on it; to Amabel Baraclough, Henry Dawson, Rebecca Dawson, Tom Dawson, Sandra Dawson, and Tristram Stuart, all of whom helped me with my Homework; to Mary Chamberlain, whose copyediting was as acute as it was gentle; and to Cindy Chan at Pan Macmillan, who could not have been a kinder, more efficient or sustaining editor.

This book was written, despite their best efforts to prevent it, amid the bustle of my daughters, and to the bovine soundtrack of the breast-pump. It is thanks to them that I found peace, and to them therefore that I dedicate these pages.